COOL FACTS

ROCKS AND MINERALS

Written by Anna Claybourne
Illustrated by Michael Posen

p

This is a Parragon Book
This edition published in 2001

Parragon
Queen Street House
4 Queen Street
Bath BA1 1HE, UK

ISBN 0-75255-407-7

Printed in Dubai

Produced by
Monkey Puzzle Media Ltd
Gissing's Farm
Fressingfield
Suffolk IP21 5SH
UK

Cover produced by David West Children's Books

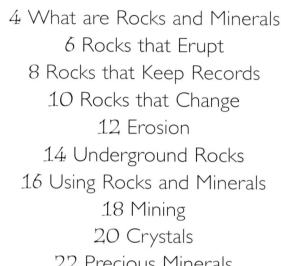

Contents

4 What are Rocks and Minerals
6 Rocks that Erupt
8 Rocks that Keep Records
10 Rocks that Change
12 Erosion
14 Underground Rocks
16 Using Rocks and Minerals
18 Mining
20 Crystals
22 Precious Minerals
24 Fuel and Power
26 Health and Medicine
28 Everyday Minerals
30 Measuring Minerals
32 Index

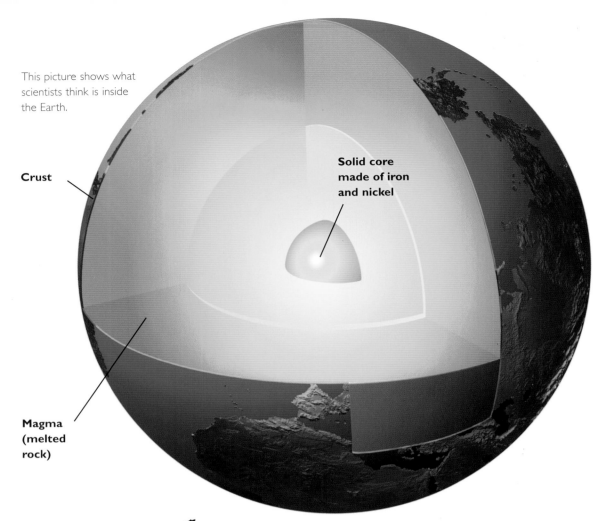

This picture shows what scientists think is inside the Earth.

Crust

Solid core made of iron and nickel

Magma (melted rock)

What are rocks?

ROCKS FORM THE HARD OUTER CRUST OF OUR PLANET, THE EARTH. ROCKS ARE made up of minerals, and minerals themselves are made up of elements. Unlike animals and plants, rocks are not alive. But that does not mean they always stay the same – in fact, they are changing all the time. Rocks can dissolve, melt, fall apart and even change into other rocks.

What are elements?
Elements are simple chemical substances such as gold and oxygen. They are the building blocks of most other substances. In fact, most things, including rocks, minerals, animals, plants, people, water and air, are made up of combinations of elements.

Is the whole of the Earth made of rocks?
Yes – you could say the Earth is one gigantic rock! But the kind of rock we are used to seeing is only on the outside, or crust. Where this crust forms the Earth's continents, the most common rock is granite.

What is the difference between a rock and a mineral?
The main difference is that a mineral is 'homogeneous' – it is the same all the way through. If you look at a lump of salt under a microscope, every part of it has the same structure. But rock is not homogeneous, it is a mixture. For example, granite, a rock, is made up of three minerals, mica, feldspar and quartz.

How can animals and plants be rocks and minerals?
Substances like chalk, coal and oil were formed millions of years ago when plants or tiny sea creatures got squashed under layers of mud and water, and eventually turned into stone. Some scientists say that things which were once alive are not true minerals. But you will find them in most books on rocks and minerals – including this one!

What is under the Earth's crust?

Just under the Earth's crust is a layer of incredibly hot, melted rock called magma. As you get nearer to the centre, or core, of the Earth, the rock gets hotter and hotter. Scientists think there is a metallic ball at the core of the Earth made of two elements, iron and nickel.

How do rocks get here from outer space?

Sometimes bits of rock from space, called meteors, get so close to the Earth that they are sucked in by gravity. Most burn up as they zoom through the Earth's atmosphere. But those that land can make a huge crater when they hit the ground.

What are minerals?

PEOPLE USE THE WORD MINERAL TO MEAN DIFFERENT THINGS. TRUE minerals are pure, solid substances made up of crystals. Some minerals, like gold and carbon, are made of one element. Others, like salt and quartz, are made of a combination of elements. Only natural substances are true minerals. So if you find some salt in a salt mine, it is a mineral, but if you make salt in a science laboratory, it is not — even though they are exactly the same!

A meteor whizzing towards the Earth would look something like this.

Some volcanoes shoot fountains of hot melted rock into the air.

When can you see rocks being made?

THE RED-HOT, STICKY LAVA THAT FLOWS FROM AN ERUPTING VOLCANO IS IN fact melted rock, or magma, from inside the Earth. As the lava cools down in the air – or sometimes in the sea – it forms solid rocks. Rocks that are made in this way, such as basalt, obsidian and pumice, are called igneous rocks (igneous means fiery). Many different kinds of igneous rocks are formed, depending on how fast the lava cools and what minerals it contains.

Which rock can float in water?

The only rock that floats in water is pumice – a type of igneous rock. It is made out of frothy lava full of gas bubbles. As it cools, the bubbles get trapped, creating very light rock. Pumice is rough, like sandpaper, so people use it for scrubbing dead skin off their feet.

How hot is melted rock?

Very hot! The temperature of magma even below the Earth's crust is over 1,500° C (2,732° F). That is 15 times hotter than boiling water (100° C or 212° F) and 40 times hotter than your body temperature (37° C or 98.6°F).

What causes a volcano?

A VOLCANO IS CAUSED BY PRESSURE BUILDING UP INSIDE THE EARTH.
This pressure causes the red-hot magma to burst out of a weak spot in the Earth's crust, along with hot gas and ash. No one knows exactly why the pressure builds up. It is probably because the rocks that make up the Earth's crust are always shifting slowly around and pressing their enormous weight against each other.

What is the most dangerous science?
Vulcanology – the study of volcanoes – is extremely dangerous. Vulcanologists have to work on active volcanoes, taking measurements and collecting rock samples. They wear fireproof suits and always work in pairs, but many of them are killed doing their job.

Where did lava make stepping stones for a giant?
The Giant's Causeway, in Ireland, got its name because according to legend it was built by a giant. In fact it was made out of a type of lava. After the lava came out of the ground, it slowly cooled and formed huge, six-sided rock pillars that look like giant stepping-stones.

The "stepping stones" in the Giant's Causeway are wider than dinner tables.

Are there volcanoes under the ground?
Sometimes hot magma from inside the Earth rises towards the surface, but never gets there. Instead it squeezes into gaps between other rocks and cools down, forming rocks like granite and dolerite. These are found in flat layers called sills, columns called dykes, or huge chunks called batholiths.

How can underground rocks build towers?
Volcanoes can erupt many times, but in the end they become "extinct". When this happens, the magma in the middle of the volcano cools into a column of hard rock. Over thousands of years, the rest of the volcano gets worn away, leaving just the central tower of rock.

How do desert roses grow?

Not many roses grow in the desert – except ones made out of rock. They grow when mineral crystals (see page 20) form between grains of sand, gluing them together in petal shapes. They are a kind of sedimentary rock.

How can we tell where the sea used to be?

We can tell from rocks and fossils, of course! Some sedimentary rocks, such as chalk and shelly limestone, form only in the sea. So we know that places where they are found were once under water. These rocks may also contain fossils of sea creatures.

A desert rose looks like a real rose made of stone.

How can mud turn to rock?

MUD THAT IS WASHED INTO THE SEA SLOWLY SETTLES ON THE SEA-BED.
More layers of mud land on top of it, and get squashed down by the weight of the water. Eventually, over thousands of years, the mud hardens into solid rock. Rock that forms in this way is called sedimentary rock. Sediment is anything that settles and collects on the ground or sea-bed. Any kind of sediment – mud, sand, shells, bits of minerals, or the remains of plants and animals – can become sedimentary rock.

Why are some rocks stripy?

Some rocks are made from layers of different-coloured sedimentary rocks. There might be layers of shale made from mud, sandstone made from sand, and coal made from rotting trees. The different layers or stripes show whether the land was a forest, a beach, or under water when the layer was formed.

What is a nodule?

Nodule just means lump. Many sedimentary rocks contain nodules, or lumps, of a completely different rock or mineral. Chalk contains nodules of a hard mineral called flint, which ancient peoples collected to make knives and axes.

How are animal fossils made?

Fossils form after an animal dies and its skeleton gets covered by sediment such as mud or sand. The sediment gradually turns into rock, while the skeleton rots away. The space left behind is slowly filled in by other rocks or minerals.

Which rocks contain the most fossils?

The quicker a dead plant or animal is buried in sediment, the more likely it is to become a fossil. So the largest numbers of fossils are found in sedimentary rocks that form quickly – such as chalk, which is made from the shells of tiny sea creatures falling to the sea-bed.

How can rocks keep records?

BECAUSE THEY ARE FULL OF FOSSILS! FOSSILS ARE THE SHAPES LEFT behind in rocks by animals and plants that died a long time ago. In layers of sedimentary rock, the oldest fossils are usually found in the lowest layers. By studying these fossils, scientists can work out how long ago animals such as dinosaurs were alive. This arrangement of fossils is such a good way of storing information that it is called the Fossil Record.

A fossilized *Gosiutichthys parvus* fish which was alive 48 million years ago.

Folded layers of rock are often easy to spot in a cliff face.

Can rocks be folded in half?
The pressure on the Earth's crust is sometimes strong enough to make rocks fold up. This can best be seen in places where stripy layers of rock have folded into curves and ripples. To see how this happens, put a piece of kitchen foil flat on a table and push it inwards from both sides.

How do rocks change into other rocks?

ROCKS CHANGE INTO OTHER ROCKS IF THEY ARE SQUEEZED EXTREMELY hard. You could not change a rock much by squeezing it with your hand. But when movements in the Earth's crust grind rocks together, the enormous pressure forms new minerals. Rocks that have been changed are called metamorphic rocks. For example, when mudstone gets squeezed, it turns into the metamorphic rock called schist, containing sparkling crystals of a mineral called mica.

How can rocks move mountains?

Sometimes rocks get squeezed together so tightly that

they can't be squeezed any more. Instead, they are forced upwards, pressing the Earth's crust into rows of mountains. The tallest mountains in the world, the Himalayas, were made in this way. They are up to 8,848 m (29,029 ft) high. As you can imagine, there is a lot of metamorphic rock in the Himalayas.

The Taj Mahal in India is a huge tomb made completely out of marble.

Which rocks make a good roof?
When a rock called shale is squeezed, it turns into slate. The squeezing makes the crystals inside the rock grow in straight lines. This is why slate breaks easily into straight, flat pieces. These rock "slices" are perfect for making roof tiles.

How do rocks get cooked?
Rocks can change their form if they get very hot – just like food. They are most likely to change if they get too close to extremely hot magma from deep inside the Earth.

Which cooked rock do sculptors like?
Marble is a kind of metamorphic rock created when limestone under the ground gets heated up by magma. Marble is usually very beautiful, with coloured streaks and swirls. It is also soft enough to be carved into sculptures and statues.

What causes earthquakes?
Scientists think the Earth's crust is made up of several massive pieces, called plates. These float on top of the hot, oozing magma inside the Earth. At the edges, the plates slowly bump and push against each other. If this pushing becomes too strong, it can cause earthquakes.

Why do fossils change shape?
When rocks get squeezed or folded, the fossils they contain can also be bent out of shape. Scientists often find stretched, twisted or crushed fossils inside metamorphic rocks.

How does a rock perform a balancing act?

Balancing rocks like this one look as though you could easily push them over!

S OMETIMES A MELTING GLACIER OR AN ERUPTING VOLCANO WILL MOVE A hard boulder on to the top of an area of softer rock. Wind and rain wear away the soft rock much faster than the hard boulder. But the boulder protects the column of rock directly beneath it. So it ends up balancing on a thin, rocky perch. When water, wind or anything else wears away rock, it is called erosion.

Why are pebbles round?
Rocks in rivers are rolled along by the current, and those in the sea are flung ashore by the waves. Pebbles are just rocks which have been bashed against each other in this way so much that their corners and rough edges have all worn away.

What is soft but can cut through rock?

THE ANSWER TO THIS RIDDLE IS WATER. YOU MIGHT NOT REALISE HOW strong water is, but just think how easily it dissolves hard grains of salt, or cuts a path through sand or mud. If it has enough time, water can do the same to rock. As a river flows, it carries away tiny particles of rock from its banks and bed. Over thousands of years, this can carve away a deep channel called a gorge.

How can mountains grow and shrink at the same time?
At the same time as wind and rain are wearing them down, many mountains are still being pushed upwards by the squeezing of the Earth's massive plates. For example, even though the Himalayas are being worn away by erosion, they are still growing by about five millimetres every year!

The Grand Canyon in America is one of the biggest gorges in the world.

How can rain eat rocks?
Rain is not pure water. It is slightly acid, because it dissolves chemicals from the air. This means that it can slowly dissolve rock. Acid rain, which has extra acid in it from polluted air, can eat the nose off a stone statue in just a few years.

Why do mountains get smaller?
With the rain dissolving their rocks and the wind wearing them away, mountains get worn down as they get older. You can often tell really old mountains, such as the Appalachians in North America, because they have a flattened, rounded shape. Younger mountains, like the Andes in South America, are more pointed.

Why is the wind good at carving?
In deserts, strong winds can carve rocks into weird and wonderful shapes. The wind does this by blowing grains of sand at the rock. The grinding action of these grains makes the rock wear away in amazing patterns.

A geyser
shooting out a
jet of boiling water.

What is a geyser?

In some places around the world, hot rocks heat up underground water so much that it shoots up out of the ground in a boiling-hot fountain. This is called a geyser. Old Faithful, a geyser in Yellowstone National Park, USA, has erupted roughly every seventy-six minutes for the last eighty years.

How can rock act like a sponge?

SOME ROCK CAN SOAK UP WATER, JUST LIKE A SPONGE. IT CAN DO THIS because it is full of tiny cracks or holes. Rocks that can hold water – such as chalk, limestone and basalt – are called permeable rocks. When it rains, water soaks down through the soil and into underground permeable rocks. Water stored there can be collected with wells and pumps.

Where does an oasis get its water?

A lush, green oasis can appear in a desert where there is little rain. Rain falls a long way away, soaks into permeable rocks and spreads out beneath the desert. Where the rocks come to the surface, fresh water springs out of the ground to form the oasis.

Where is the world's biggest cave system?

Caves are very hard to measure, and we might not have discovered them all yet! Mammoth-Flint Ridge Cave System in central Kentucky, USA, is the longest cave system ever explored, with 550 km (342 miles) of underground passages, chambers and lakes.

What are stalactites and stalagmites?

As water drips from the ceiling of a limestone cave, it leaves a tiny deposit of limestone on the ceiling and a second deposit where it lands. Over thousands of years, these deposits build up into spikes of rock which look like icicles. Stalactites hang down from the ceiling. Stalagmites stick up from the ground.

What melts the ice in Iceland?

In Iceland, hot magma inside the Earth heats up underground rocks. When water gets into cracks between these rocks, it boils. People pump out this boiling water and use it to heat their houses.

How are caves formed?

MANY CAVES ARE FORMED WHEN WATER UNDER the ground eats away at rocks such as limestone over thousands of years. Limestone is easily dissolved by the small amount of acid in rainwater. Cracks in the limestone gradually get bigger and bigger, until they turn into caves and tunnels. When the water level drops, air fills the newly formed cave.

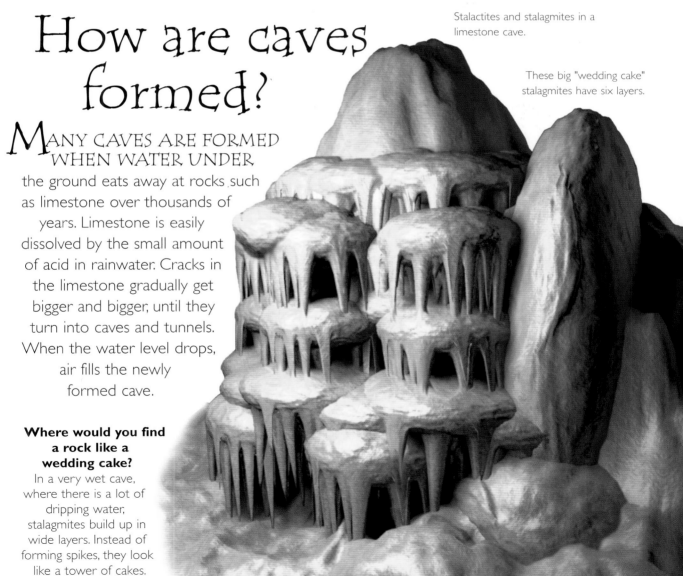

Stalactites and stalagmites in a limestone cave.

These big "wedding cake" stalagmites have six layers.

Where would you find a rock like a wedding cake?

In a very wet cave, where there is a lot of dripping water, stalagmites build up in wide layers. Instead of forming spikes, they look like a tower of cakes.

This lump of granite could be turned into a work surface or even a statue.

An Iron Age sword, made from iron studded with precious minerals.

What are rocks and minerals used for?

Rocks and minerals have millions of different uses. We use them to make coins, knives and forks, spectacles, aeroplanes, frying pans, toothpaste, roads, buildings, computers and many other things. As well as being useful, some of them are very valuable. Precious stones such as diamonds make lots of money for the people who find them.

Where can I see rocks and minerals being used?
Just look out of the window. The window itself is made from limestone (a rock) and quartz (a mineral). The cars driving past and the bricks of your house come from rocks or minerals. So do many things inside the house, including plastic toys, colouring pens, CDs, dinner plates and jewellery.

When did people first use rocks?
Rocks were probably the first tools people ever used – for cracking nuts open, or bashing a fish or rabbit over the head for food. Over time, people learned to cut rock into bricks, and to cut or melt different minerals out of rocks.

Are metals minerals?
Metals are one of the most important and useful types of mineral. Metals are perfect for making things, because they are strong and flexible, and can be melted down and poured into moulds. Some important metals, such as uranium, have to be extracted from other minerals.

Can we eat minerals?
Only a few minerals are edible. You might know the mineral called halite by another name – table salt. Vitamin pills sometimes contain minerals we need, such as iron. But there are other minerals, such as yellow orpiment, which are deadly poisonous.

Could we live without minerals?

No, our bodies need minerals such as iron, calcium and zinc in order to work properly. We usually get them from food – for example, spinach contains iron. Life would also be hard without metal tools, computers and all the other things we make out of minerals.

Can we make our own minerals?

Scientists can copy some minerals in the laboratory, and make their own versions using chemical reactions. But these are not true minerals, because they are not natural. There are some minerals, such as gold, that no one can make. But many people have tried!

Crystals of the mineral halite, otherwise known as table salt.

How many kinds of minerals are there?

THERE ARE ABOUT 3,000 DIFFERENT minerals – but most of them are very rare. We only use a few hundred of them to make things. Minerals are usually found in rocks, mixed together with other minerals, so it is not always easy to tell which is which. Scientists called mineralogists collect them and make lists of all the different types. Lots of minerals have long, strange names – like skutterudite, demantoid and kornerupine!

How do we extract minerals from rocks?

Metals such as copper, tin and silver can be melted out of the rock in which they are trapped. To extract precious stones such as diamonds, the rock is crushed and the harder gems inside are left whole. Salt is extracted by pumping water into the ground, so that the salt dissolves. The salty water is collected and heated, and as it evaporates pure salt is left behind. Other minerals have to be extracted using complicated chemical reactions.

What is an ore?

An ore is any type of rock or mineral that contains something useful that we want to extract. For example, haematite is an iron ore. It is a mineral made up of iron and oxygen, and we extract iron from it. Before extracting minerals from ores, we have to get the ores out of the ground. This is usually done by mining.

Is mining dangerous?

Mining used to be extremely dangerous, because miners had to crawl under ground and use picks to dig out the ores. Today, the use of machines has made mining safer. But there is still a risk from mines collapsing, gas exploding, and accidents with machines.

Why do minerals get mixed up together?

Minerals often grow inside rocks or other minerals, so they are mixed up to start with. When the huge plates on the Earth's surface push against each other, the pressure muddles up the rocks and minerals even more.

A lump of the mineral haematite, a type of iron ore, clinging to a rock.

What are prospectors?

Prospectors are people who search for valuable minerals. They usually have a lot of knowledge about the best places to find them. Prospectors can earn a lot of money by discovering gold, oil or diamonds.

What was the Gold Rush?

In 1848, gold was discovered in California, on the west coast of the USA. Thousands of people from all over the country, and from other parts of the world, rushed to the area to look for gold. The lucky ones got rich, but many others found nothing.

How do you pan for gold?

Panning is a way of collecting the tiny gold nuggets that are sometimes found on river beds. You put a handful of sand or gravel from the river bed in a shallow pan and swirl it around. If there are any bits of gold, they sink to the bottom because gold is so heavy.

Treasure hunters panning for gold during the California Gold Rush.

Where should you look for minerals?

Minerals often collect near "plate boundaries", the edges of the big plates that make up the Earth's crust. For example, California and Peru are both near big plate boundaries, and they are famous for metals like gold and copper. Scientists can find out exactly where minerals are by measuring how magnetic the ground is, or how fast shock waves pass through it.

Rose quartz is a type of quartz crystal with a pale pink colour.

What is a crystal?

THE WORD CRYSTAL MAKES US THINK OF A SYMMETRICAL, TRANSPARENT OBJECT with smooth sides and sharp angles – like a diamond or quartz. In fact, nearly all rocks and minerals are made up of crystals. The tiny atoms that form minerals are arranged in regular patterns, which means that most minerals will grow in crystal shapes if they have enough space.

How can you make a crystal disappear?
If you put a cryolite crystal in a glass of water, you won't be able to see it! This is because cryolite bends light in exactly the same way water does. So when the cryolite crystal is in water, it looks just like water.

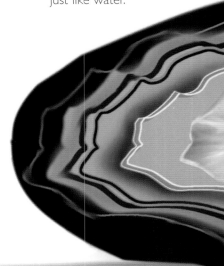

Can crystals glow in the dark?
Several minerals, such as willemite and datolite, continue to give off a pale glow for a few minutes after a light is switched off. They have a very important use – they are used to make glow-in-the-dark paint!

Why don't all minerals form perfect crystals?
For a mineral to form a perfect crystal, it has to have enough space to grow freely. Crystals can form in liquid lava as it cools after coming out of a volcano. Others grow in water that contains dissolved minerals. But it is harder for minerals to grow into crystal shapes if they are trapped inside solid rock.

"Hair pyrites", or millerite crystals, growing on a rock.

Are crystals all the same shape?

No, there are seven basic shapes of crystal. The shape is created by the pattern in which the crystal's atoms are joined together. For example, crystals of pyrite are shaped like a cube.

Can crystals tell the time?

You have probably heard of quartz watches. Quartz is a very hard mineral, with crystals that vibrate very fast when electricity is applied to them. The vibrations are so precise and regular that they can be used to count seconds, minutes and hours.

Which crystals look like hair?

Millerite crystals are so long and narrow that they resemble hair. Because of this, millerite is also called "hair pyrites". But the crystals are not soft like hair – they are hard and brittle.

What is a thunder egg?

A THUNDER EGG IS ANOTHER NAME FOR A GEODE – A HOLLOW ROCK full of transparent crystals. A geode starts off as a bubble of water or air trapped inside rock. The bubble slowly fills up with minerals dissolved in water, and they form crystals around the inside of the bubble. The rest of the rock gets worn away, leaving an "egg" full of crystals.

This geode has been cut in half so you can see the crystals inside it.

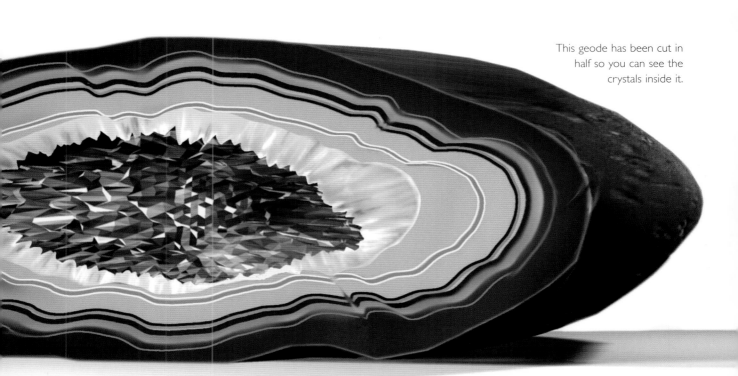

Asterism makes this ruby sparkle in a star-shaped pattern.

Which metal is the most precious?

When you think of a precious metal, you probably think of gold. But platinum is even more precious than gold, and much rarer. If you were lucky enough to collect all the platinum ever extracted from the Earth, it would fit inside a room only 8m x 8m (27ft x 27ft).

Which gemstones are the most valuable?

The most precious gemstones are diamonds, emeralds and rubies. The price of precious stones depends on how many have been found, how many people want to buy them, and how perfect they are. Diamonds are very popular, but a perfect, flawless emerald could cost more than a diamond of the same size.

What do diamonds and coal have in common?

Diamonds and coal are made of the same thing – an element called carbon. If it is compressed and heated to very high temperatures, carbon can form into diamonds. Scientists think diamond crystals are formed in melted rock, deep inside the Earth, which is why they are much harder to find than coal.

Which mineral can make a fool of you?

If you discovered iron pyrites, you might think you had struck gold. But although it looks like gold, iron pyrites is not very precious. It is a common mineral made of iron and sulphur. So many people have been fooled by it that iron pyrites is known as "fool's gold".

Which gemstones can make you a star?

Some rubies and sapphires reflect light in a star-shaped pattern. This is known as asterism, and it adds value to a precious stone. Asterism is caused by tiny bubbles of gas that became trapped inside the mineral as it formed.

How did a pebble lead to a fortune?

IN SOUTH AFRICA IN 1866, A BOY CALLED ERASMUS JACOBS FOUND A BEAUTIFUL white pebble in a stream on his father's farm. A visitor spotted the pebble and took it to be examined by scientists. It turned out to be a diamond. The find led to the discovery and opening of the world's biggest diamond mines, in a place called Kimberley.

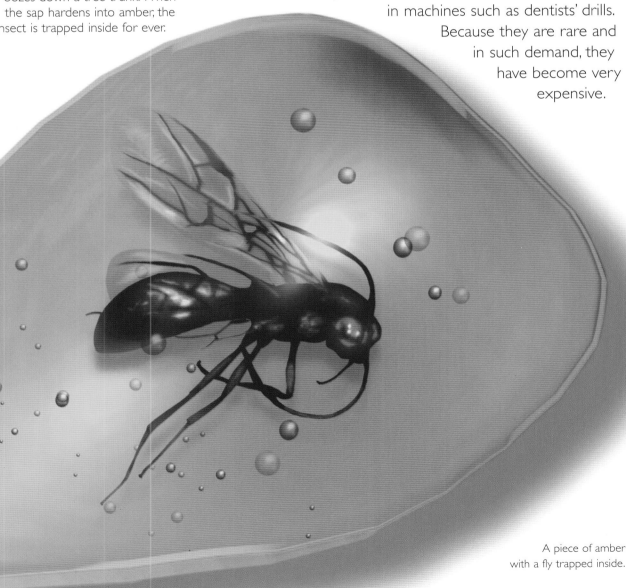

Why doesn't the world's biggest diamond sparkle?

The world's biggest diamond, called the Star of Africa, is part of the Crown Jewels which belong to the British royal family. It does not sparkle as much as it could, because it was cut before diamond-cutting techniques were perfected. Today, an expert cutter can make a diamond sparkle when seen from any angle.

How do flies get trapped in amber?

Amber is a kind of precious stone made of hardened sap, which is the sticky fluid flowing inside a tree. Insects often get caught in sap as it oozes down a tree trunk. When the sap hardens into amber, the insect is trapped inside for ever.

Why are some minerals so valuable?

CERTAIN MINERALS BECOME VALUABLE USUALLY BECAUSE THEY ARE beautiful, rare and long-lasting. Gold, for example, is a pure metal that does not react with other chemicals. This means it won't rot or rust away. Diamonds are lovely to look at, and they are also extremely hard. So, as well as being cut into beautiful shapes to make jewellery, diamonds are used in machines such as dentists' drills. Because they are rare and in such demand, they have become very expensive.

A piece of amber with a fly trapped inside.

Where did coal and oil get their energy?

ALL FUELS WERE ONCE LIVING THINGS. COAL IS MAINLY THE FOSSILIZED remains of trees that lived millions of years ago. They lived by converting the sun's power into chemical energy. Petroleum oil is the fossilized remains of tiny sea creatures, which lived by converting food into chemical energy. When these trees and creatures died, the chemical energy stored in their cells remained. By burning coal and petroleum oil, we can release this energy to heat our homes and power our cars.

Are fossil fuels really minerals?

The word mineral is sometimes used for anything obtained through mining. Like all true minerals, fossil fuels are homogeneous (see page 4) and occur naturally. But scientists say that only materials which have never been alive can be true minerals.

What else can coal and oil be used for?

Oil is made into plastic, one of the most useful substances in the world. Think of all the plastic things in your house, from toys to telephones to toilet brushes. Wax crayons, non-stick surfaces, polystyrene, sticky tape, detergent and nylon are all made from oil too. Coal is used in ink, soap, fertilizers and nail polish.

Will oil and coal supplies last for ever?

It has been estimated that we will use up all the Earth's oil in the next fifty years, and all the coal in 200 years! Scientists are studying the best ways to collect energy from the wind; the movement of rivers, waterfalls and waves; and the Sun.

An oil rig in the ocean collects oil from under the sea-bed.

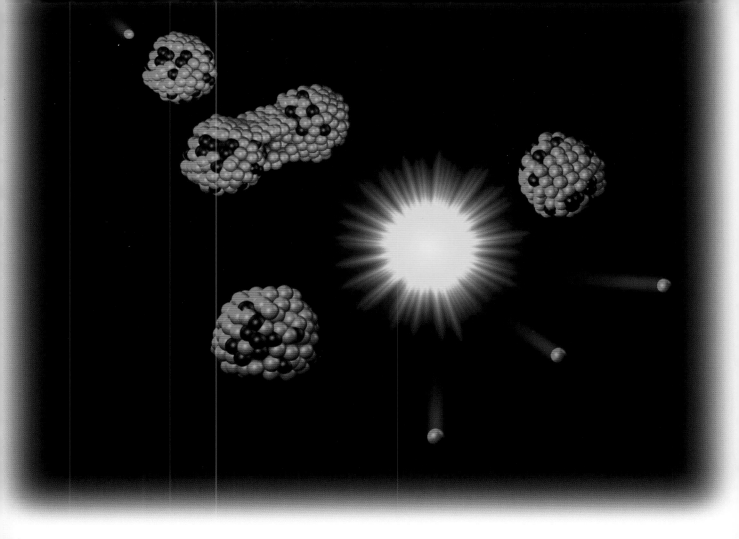

In this nuclear fission reaction, atoms of uranium are being split apart.

What is radiation?

Radiation is a kind of energy that comes from atoms – the tiny particles that make up elements. Some atoms are unstable. This makes them give out radiation, which is used in X-rays, nuclear power-stations, and bombs. Uranium is one of the main radioactive elements, and can be found in the minerals uranophane and pitchblende.

How does nuclear power work?

Nuclear power works by either splitting apart unstable atoms (fission), or joining them together (fusion). That is what happens inside nuclear power-stations. Both these processes create huge amounts of energy which we can convert into useful power.

Does a nuclear bomb work in the same way?

Yes, it uses nuclear fission or fusion. But instead of creating a steady flow of useful energy, the nuclear reaction in a bomb is designed to happen very fast. As each atom is split or joined it causes a chain reaction in other atoms, creating a massive explosion of heat and light.

Which mineral do people fight wars over?

Petroleum oil provides fuel for aeroplanes and cars. The world would soon grind to a halt without it. This makes it very valuable, and several countries have fought wars over areas of land that contain oil. In the Gulf War of 1990–91, Iraq invaded its smaller neighbour Kuwait, hoping to capture its oil-rich land. Countries such as the USA helped to defend Kuwait, because of their interest in its oil supplies.

What minerals does my body need?

YOUR BODY NEEDS ABOUT EIGHTY MINERAL SUBSTANCES. THAT IS too many to list here, but some of the main ones are copper, zinc, potassium, iron (good for your blood), calcium (good for your bones), fluorine (for healthy teeth), and iodine (without it you get a lumpy neck!). We don't have to dig these minerals out of the ground to eat them. They are usually found in tiny amounts in our food, mixed in with other chemicals.

How can you become partly mineral?

You already are, because of all the minerals your body takes out of the food you eat. But if any of your bones or joints were damaged, you could become even more mineral – by having them replaced with titanium, a metal that comes from minerals found in the ground.

Does everyone need the same minerals?

It depends a bit on who you are. For example, everyone needs a bit of salt, but too much salt can be bad for people with heart problems.

Are there really minerals in mineral water?

Yes. Mineral water that you buy in a bottle has usually been collected from a natural, underground spring. It has been filtered through layers of rock, gradually dissolving small amounts of minerals. Sometimes these are good for you and sometimes they just make the water taste nice.

Can minerals treat diseases?

Yes, one of the most important mineral treatments is chemotherapy, which is used to treat cancer. Chemotherapy drugs are made from minerals like barite and platinum.

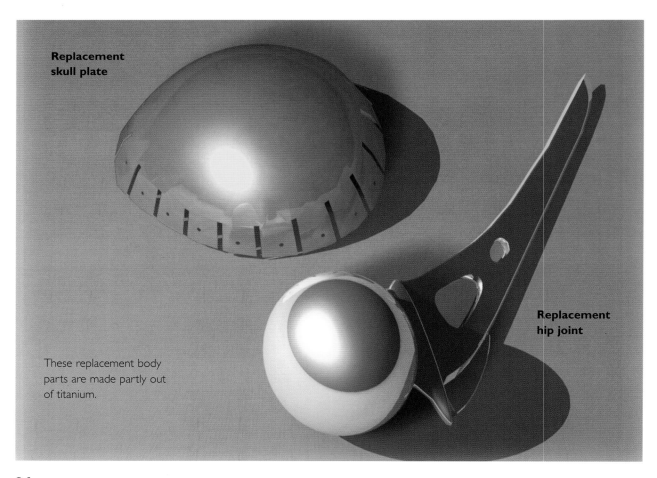

Replacement skull plate

Replacement hip joint

These replacement body parts are made partly out of titanium.

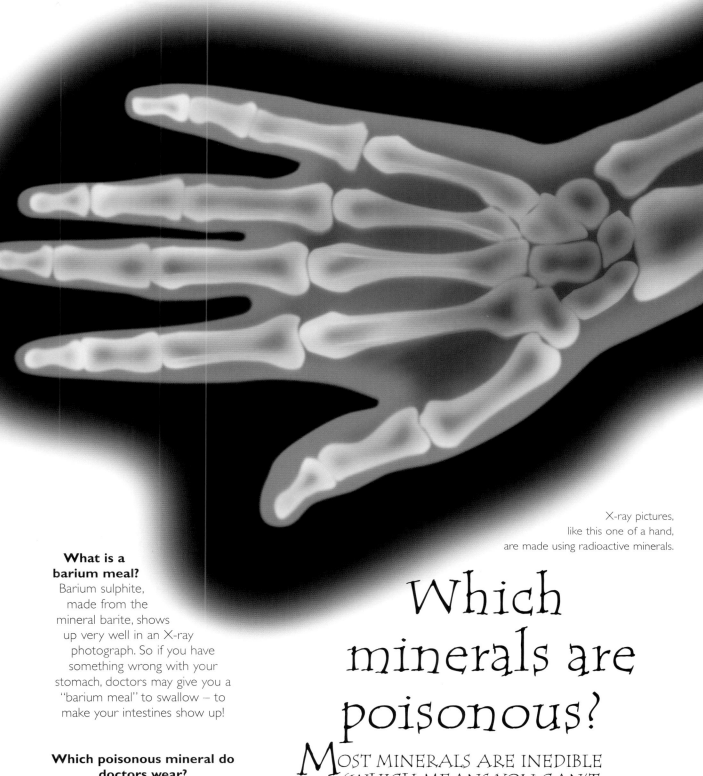

X-ray pictures, like this one of a hand, are made using radioactive minerals.

What is a barium meal?

Barium sulphite, made from the mineral barite, shows up very well in an X-ray photograph. So if you have something wrong with your stomach, doctors may give you a "barium meal" to swallow – to make your intestines show up!

Which poisonous mineral do doctors wear?

Lead may be poisonous to eat, but it also saves doctors from radiation poisoning. X-rays work by sending a small amount of radiation through your body. Radiation is dangerous in large amounts. Lead stops radiation in its tracks, so doctors who work with X-rays every day wear lead in protective clothing.

Which minerals are poisonous?

MOST MINERALS ARE INEDIBLE (WHICH MEANS YOU CAN'T eat them), but some are also deadly poisonous. These include lead, mercury and orpiment. Orpiment contains arsenic, a famous poison that was once used to kill rats. Other minerals, such as asbestos, are poisonous if you breathe in their dust. Even essential minerals are bad for you if you have too much of them. Your body needs copper, but a large amount would make you very ill.

Are there minerals in my bathroom?

YOUR BATHROOM IS A GREAT PLACE TO SPOT MINERALS.

Talcum powder is made of talc, a common mineral extracted from huge mines in America. Do you have a sea-shell soap dish? It is made of calcium carbonate minerals, collected from the sea by the creature that used to live in it. Shampoo and bubble bath contain minerals like sodium and sulphur, and the mirror is made of glass (made from quartz), backed with a thin layer of silver.

Is the lead in a pencil really lead?

No, it is a different mineral called graphite. Like coal and diamonds, graphite is made out of carbon. It is not poisonous, so sucking your pencil will not give you lead poisoning.

How can a mineral take a photograph?

The film in a camera is coated with chemicals that change when light hits them. The main one is silver halide, made out of silver. Silver is not the only precious metal to have unusual uses – platinum is used to make tongs for chemists, and gold is sometimes used to make false teeth.

What minerals make a light bulb work?

When you switch on a light, electricity flows along copper wires and into a filament made of tungsten (which comes from a mineral called wolframite). The filament glows and shines through a light bulb of glass (made from quartz). Mineral teamwork!

Am I wearing any minerals?

Apart from the plastic, metal and quartz in your watch, the glass in your glasses, and the gold or silver in your ear-rings, you are probably wearing a synthetic fabric like nylon or polyester in your clothes or shoes. Nylon and polyester are made from mineral oil.

Nylon combat trousers and plastic-soled trainers are both made using minerals.

How many more uses do minerals have?

X-rays, medicines, computers, watches, plastics, fuels and jewels – you have already seen a lot of the useful things minerals are used for. But there are many, many more. In fact, minerals have so many uses they would not all fit in this book.

How can minerals show me the way home?

A compass contains a magnetized steel needle, which always points north because it is attracted by the Earth's magnetism. Steel is made from the mineral iron, and magnetism was first discovered in a magnetic mineral called lodestone.

The needle in this compass is swinging around to point northwards.

Will computers replace minerals?

No – BECAUSE THEY DEPEND ON THEM TO WORK. YOU have probably heard of silicon chips, which are used in computers and calculators. Silicon comes from quartz, which is one of the most common minerals on Earth. As well as being found in rocks, quartz is the main ingredient of sand.

How do you identify a mineral?

YOU CAN TEST THE HARDNESS OF A MINERAL BY SEEING WHAT WILL

scratch it – talc can be scratched with your fingernail and apatite can be scratched with a penknife, but a diamond can only be scratched by another diamond. You can divide the weight by the volume to measure a mineral's density. Its colour, shape and smell can also help. Scientists have huge books with details and photographs of every mineral, so they can look each specimen up.

How do scientists measure minerals?

Scientists usually measure minerals by their hardness and by their density (how heavy they are for their size). Precious stones and metals can also be measured in carats.

What is a carat?

Carat has two meanings. For measuring precious stones, such as diamonds, a carat is 0.2 g. So a diamond that weighs 1 g is a 5-carat diamond. For precious metals, the carat (or karat) shows how pure the metal is. Gold, for example, is often mixed with other metals to make it cheaper. One carat stands for 1/24 of the mixture. So 18-carat gold is 18/24 gold, and 24-carat gold is pure gold.

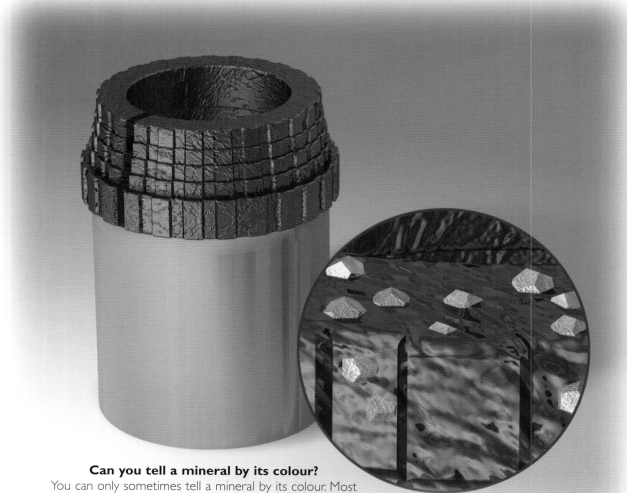

Can you tell a mineral by its colour?

You can only sometimes tell a mineral by its colour. Most people think sapphires are blue, but they can also be white, yellow or pink. Mineralogists often have to use several different methods before they can identify a mineral properly.

A diamond-tipped drill used for boring into the ground.

Chrsocolla

Why are diamonds used for cutting?

Diamond is the hardest of all materials, and it can cut through most other things easily. That is why it is used to make drills. So how are diamonds themselves cut? They can be split in half by giving them a knock with a hammer, or cut using another diamond or a laser.

Why do some minerals smell?

Minerals usually smell because they react with the air or with water to produce a gas, which you can smell as it wafts away. For example, minerals that contain sulphur often smell like rotten eggs. Minerals that contain arsenic smell a bit like garlic.

Malachite

How does a mineral make its mark?

The mark a mineral makes is called its streak, and is a good way to identify it. For example, although they look the same, iron pyrites makes a black streak, and gold makes a gold streak. Mineralogists often do a "streak test" by rubbing a mineral across the back of a plain white bathroom tile.

The three minerals on this page are all copper ores. Many minerals containing copper are blue.

Who was Doctor Mohs?

DOCTOR FRIEDRICH MOHS WAS A GERMAN mineralogist. He invented the Mohs Scale of Hardness to measure minerals. On the Mohs Scale, 1 is the softest and 10 is the hardest. Mohs added an example for each number on the scale: (1) Talc (2) Gypsum (3) Calcite (4) Fluorite (5) Apatite (6) Feldspar (7) Quartz (8) Topaz (9) Corundum (10) Diamond. Mohs also invented the system for identifying different shapes of crystal.

Peacock ore

Index

AB

acid rain 13
amber 23
apatite 30, 31
asbestos 27
asterism 22
barite 26
barium 27
basalt 6, 14

CDE

calcite 31
calcium 17, 26
carats 30
caves 14, 15
chalk 8, 9, 14
coal 8, 22, 24
copper 18, 19, 26, 27, 28
corundum 31
crust 4, 5, 6, 7, 10, 11, 19
cryolite 20
crystals 8, 10, 11, 20
datolite 20
demantoid 17
desert roses 8
diamonds 16, 18, 19, 20, 22, 23, 30, 31
dolerite 7
earthquakes 11
elements 4, 22, 25
emeralds 22
erosion 12
extraction 18, 22, 28

FGH

feldspar 31
flint 8
fluorine 26
fluorite 31
fossils 8, 9, 11, 24
gemstones 22, 30
geodes 21
geysers 14
Giant's Causeway 7
glaciers 12
gold 17, 19, 22, 23, 28, 30
gorges 13
granite 4, 7, 16
graphite 28
gypsum 31
haematite 18
hair pyrites 21

IJKL

igneous rocks 6
iodine 26
iron 16, 17, 18, 22, 26, 29
iron pyrites 22, 31
kornerupine 17
lava 6, 7
lead 27, 28
limestone 8, 11, 14, 15, 16
lodestone 29

MNO

magma 4, 5, 6, 7, 11, 15
marble 11
mercury 27
metals 16, 22, 23, 28, 30
metamorphic rocks 10, 11
meteors 5
mica 10
millerite 21
mining 18, 24, 28
Mohs Scale 31
mountains 11, 13
mud 4, 8
mudstone 10
nodules 8
nuclear power 25
oases 14
obsidian 6
oil 19, 24, 25, 28
ore 18
orpiment 16, 27

PQR

panning 19
pebbles 12, 22
permeable rocks 14
pitchblende 25
plates 11, 13, 18, 19
platinum 22, 26, 28
potassium 26
prospectors 19
pumice 6
pyrites 21
quartz 4, 5, 16, 20, 21, 28, 29, 31
radiation 25, 27
rubies 22

STU

salt 5, 16, 18, 26
sandstone 8
sapphires 22, 30
schist 10
sedimentary rocks 8, 9
shale 8, 11

silicon 29
silver 18, 28
skutterudite 17
slate 11
sodium 28
stalactites 15
stalagmites 15
sulphur 22, 28, 31
talc 28, 30, 31
thunder eggs 21
tin 18
titanium 26
tools 16, 17
topaz 31
uranium 25
uranophane 25

VWXYZ

volcanoes 6, 7, 12
water 13, 14, 15, 18, 26
willemite 20
wind 13
wolframite 28
zinc 17, 26